We Buy Food at the Store

Jayden Coll-Seck

Rosen REAL READERS

Rosen Classroom™
New York

We go to the store with Mom and Dad.

We have a list of food.

The list shows us what we need.

First, we get eggs.
We make sure that they are not broken.

Then we get milk.

Milk comes from cows.

Next, we get some cheese.

There are so many to choose from!

Then we get butter.

Butter tastes good on toast.

We get orange juice.
It is very good for you.

Then we get vegetables.
They are healthy for you.

Our shopping is done.

Time to go to the cash register!

Now we pay for the food.

Mom lets me give her credit card.

Words to Know

butter

eggs

list

orange juice